essentials

Solving Problems

Time-saving books that teach specific skills to busy people, focusing on what really matters; the things that make a difference – the *essentials*. Other books in the Essentials series include:

Making Great Presentations

Writing Good Reports

Speaking in Public

Responding to Stress

Succeeding at Interviews

Getting Started on the Internet

Hiring People

Writing Great Copy

Making the Best Man's Speech

Feeling Good for No Reason

Making the Most of Your Time

For full details please send for a free copy of the latest catalogue. See back cover for address.

The things that really matter about

Solving Problems

Steve Kneeland

ESSENTIALS

Published in 1999 by
How To Books Ltd, 3 Newtec Place,
Magdalen Road, Oxford OX4 1RE, United Kingdom
Te: (01865) 793806   Fax: (01865) 248780
email: info@howtobooks.co.uk
www.howtobooks.co.uk

British Library Cataloguing in Publication Data.
A catalogue record for this book is available from
the British Library.

Edited by Nikki Read
Cover design by Shireen Nathoo Design
Produced for How To Books by Deer Park Productions
Typeset by Euroset, Alresford, Hampshire
Printed and bound in Great Britain

NOTE: The material contained in this book is set out in good faith for
general guidance and no liability can be accepted for loss or expense
incurred as a result of relying in particular circumstances on
statements made in the book. Laws and regulations are complex and
liable to change, and readers should check the current position with
the relevant authorities before making personal arrangements.

ESSENTIALS *is an imprint of*
How To Books

Contents

Preface

Problem-solving is something that a lot of us take for granted. But most of us haven't trained ourselves to be good problem-solvers or indeed have given much thought to the problem-solving process. However the process of developing sound solutions to problems can be learned like any other skill.

Whether we are solving a problem ourselves or helping someone else solve a problem, the best place to begin is with a good practical understanding of the problem-solving process.

There are a lot of different models of the problem-solving process. The critical thing isn't having the right model. There is no such thing, each is about as good as another. The critical thing is that you have a simple model in your mind so that it becomes ingrained and used instinctively. This book delivers a simple six-step model. The first three steps have to do with defining the problem and the next three steps move us from the understanding phase into the solution phase: exploring and developing a variety of solution options and then acting upon the best one. Treat this model as a convenient checklist of basic steps needed to bring order to the problem-solving and decision-making process.

Steve Kneeland

1 Understanding the Problem

Problem–solving isn't about intelligence.
It's about thinking straight.
About getting the process right.

5
things that
really matter

1 ASSESSING THE PROBLEM

2 THINKING LOGICALLY AND CONSTRUCTIVELY

3 USING A SIX-STEP MODEL

4 CONFUSING PROBLEM-SOLVING WITH DECISION-
   MAKING

5 IT'S A LEARNING PROCESS

There is no magic formula for solving problems. The trick is to find a method that works for *you*, for the way you operate. The **key to success** is to use it consistently so that it becomes an integral part of how you think and react.

A problem is a gap between what *is* and what *ought* to be. Between the ways things are and the way you'd like them to be. They basically fall into two types.

• Fix-it problems.

• Do-it problems.

The **fix-it** problem is quite simply an **existing, unsatisfactory situation** that needs to be **fixed as soon as possible.**

The **do-it** problem is a bit different. Here we are set an **objective to achieve**. The problem is figuring out exactly how to do it.

Sometimes we have to deal with a fix-it problem as a short-term measure before deciding upon a further strategy as a do-it problem, to make sure it doesn't happen again.

IS THIS YOU?

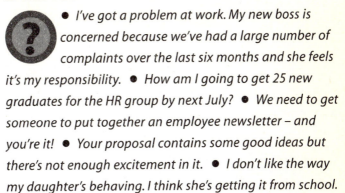

● *I've got a problem at work. My new boss is concerned because we've had a large number of complaints over the last six months and she feels it's my responsibility.* ● *How am I going to get 25 new graduates for the HR group by next July?* ● *We need to get someone to put together an employee newsletter – and you're it!* ● *Your proposal contains some good ideas but there's not enough excitement in it.* ● *I don't like the way my daughter's behaving. I think she's getting it from school.*

 ## ASSESSING THE PROBLEM

Problems come in many forms. Some are **fix-it** problems. For example:

- The number of referrals has risen to the point where we can't handle things under the current set-up.
- I think the product line is showing its age. If we don't do something soon it'll be too late.

The *gap* in both these cases is between an unsatisfactory state of affairs now and achieving a good state of affairs as soon as possible in the future. This is a **fix-it** problem that needs to be dealt with without delay.

Or it could be:

- The Nottingham branch has been given the goal of reducing inventory costs by 10%.
- My partner and I have decided to pack up smoking.

The *gap* here is between absolutely nothing and the outcome we want to achieve. These are **do-it** problems that require longer term planning where unexpected obstacles along the way might throw the unwary off course.

Fix-It problems ask you to fix it – make the problem go away.
Do-It problems ask you to do it – move us in that direction.

Having identified the problem we now ask ourselves three simple questions.

- How urgent is it?
- How important is it?
- Whose responsibility is it?

How urgent is it? Do I need to give it top priority or can I do it tomorrow? Some problems are urgent. A customer's store in Leeds has received the York delivery and vice-versa. Both store managers want things sorted by midday at the latest. This is a *fix-it* problem where you do whatever is needed to meet your customer's immediate needs.

How important is it? Urgent problems clamour for attention but it might not reflect their importance in the overall scheme of things. Do you tell your PA to lock the office door and hold all calls whilst you think about the problem or can it wait until the next meeting when you can put it against the new business plan? It now becomes a *do-it* problem.

Whose responsibility is it? It's our problem but exactly whose responsibility is it? The urgent, *fix-it* problem is satisfying the Leeds and York customers, and the *do-it* problem is making sure it doesn't happen again. You manage the process of seeing that all aspects of the problem are properly dealt with. You don't have the time to deal with it yourself.

THINKING LOGICALLY AND CONSTRUCTIVELY

You must think logically and constructively about future consequences because you can't afford the pitfalls of incorrect reactions. A major pitfall is reacting too quickly by trying to solve a problem immediately. There's nothing necessarily *wrong* with that but you mustn't expect to achieve long-term solutions immediately as well. You might have fixed the problem of getting a parcel that missed despatch to Southampton by using a special courier but you need to make sure it doesn't happen again, otherwise you fall into the pitfall of treating the symptoms of the problem instead of the cause.

Successful managers sometimes make quick decisions but they rarely make snap judgements. They might decide it's someone else's problem and organise the best-placed person to deal with it. They avoid the pitfall of assuming it's their job to deal with every problem that arises when others are more qualified to do so.

Make sure you're treating the cause and not the symptoms of the problem.

In order to think logically and constructively you need to keep things as simple as possible. The number seven is important. Seven, plus or minus two, is reportedly the number of things a human can actively keep in their head at any one time. Don't overburden your thinking processes. Information overload creates its own difficulties and you don't want them to cloud the problem-solving process.

USING A SIX-STEP MODEL

Developing a straightforward problem-solving model in your mind will help you keep things simple whilst focusing on the issues and avoiding the pitfalls. You have already embarked upon the problem-solving process by reading thus far in this book and you will soon be able to tailor the suggested model to your own experiences.

What's the single most important thing you can do to become a more effective problem-solver? Beg, borrow, steal or develop a step-by-step problem-solving model and use it until it becomes second nature.

Any model you use must be easy to recall and be flexible enough to apply to every-day situations. A six-step structure is illustrated below but a good working model should allow you to change the number and order of its steps to suit your needs.

The structure of this book is based upon our problem-solving model with Chapter 1 comprising the first step and the subsequent chapters reflecting the other five. There is considerable overlap across each of these steps and a good deal of skipping back and forth between them.

1. **Becoming aware of the problem.** Something is brought to your notice that requires your undivided attention.

2. **Gathering relevant facts.** You *investigate* the circumstances, ask a few questions where needed, and *get the facts* from the people who matter.

3. **Defining the problem.** You make sure you're *familiar* with the problem *in its entirety.* You know what it is.

4. **Developing solution options.** You decide *what* to do and *how* you're going to do it.

5. **Selecting the best solution.** You do it after making sure you have everything you need. There is nothing worse than postponing or cancelling a project through lack of information or expertise.

6. **Implementing the solution.** You look at the results to see if the problem has been *solved*.

The last step is important. It is used to check whether you need to start again with Step 1 if the problem still hasn't been resolved. This is called an *iterative* model. If you do have to go back to the beginning, make sure you include in your information any evidence of why you think the system failed to work the first time. In other words, **don't repeat mistakes you might have just made.**

 CONFUSING PROBLEM-SOLVING WITH DECISION-MAKING

Because these are often inter-linked many people think they mean the same but they are actually quite different. A problem for many can arise from a poor decision, often made elsewhere, and an incorrect decision is easily made if a problem isn't assessed properly. Imagine a situation where you have to make a decision between Mike and Ruth for promotion to a higher level job. Both are excellent candidates and deserve the opportunity. Who gets the job? What do you do with the loser?

- A **problem** is a gap between the way things are and the way they ought to be. **Problem-solving** is often about things that have already happened.

- A **decision** is a choice between two or more alternatives. **Decision-making** focuses on building and shaping the future. It is often the province of more senior levels of management.

Similarly, there can be some confusion between the two when dealing with an urgent problem. With the Leeds and York store managers demanding action, a **do-it decision** has to be made to prevent further **fix-it problems** occurring again.

With every new challenge comes the need for a workable method to complete it successfully.

You must remember that when tough decisions are made you are often effectively telling someone *it's your problem – deal with it!* That's OK providing you ensure your team is geared up to tackle it. It's a fact that many of today's problems are generated by poor decision-making coupled, inevitably, with ineffectual management practice. A bad decision now generates problems which, in turn, create inefficient working practices, and perhaps even major crises, further down the line. How much better it is for you to get it right first time.

In the same way as poor tradesmen blame their tools for poor workmanship, poor managers blame their teams for not hitting targets.

 IT'S A LEARNING PROCESS

Practising managers will tell you they don't bother with a problem-solving model but still sing its praises as a useful tool for their team to use. They might not use it *consciously* but the chances are they do, as part of their day-to-day routine.

With every new **challenge** comes the need for a workable method to complete it successfully. Don't worry if you don't realise you're using it. That's good. It means you've acquired new skills that are now an *integral part* of your working practice. The challenge, in becoming more effective as problem-solvers, is that of starting with a stepwise model of the basic problem-solving process. Then, whilst recognising its limitations, keep it in the background, *adapt* it to the realities of the situation and understand where and how it can be *best used* in practice.

You need to keep your antenna up. One of the biggest challenges as a manager is to avoid getting tied up in too many meetings, becoming weighed down by the papers in your in-tray or diligently reading through a 30-page report.

Every new challenge can be met with a tried and tested method to approach it.

It's much better to learn of problems before they appear in a pile of reports by circulating and asking colleagues face to face how things are going. Probe for that extra bit of information if the answer is not quite as it should have been. High level executives call this *sampling* their colleagues' thinking to check everything is under control.

For the same reason you should stay close to the customer, because it's better to hear through the grapevine that they are talking to another supplier than it is to discover, two months later, a sudden drop in orders in that account.

MAKING WHAT MATTERS WORK FOR YOU

✓ Assess the problem. Is it a fix-it or a do-it problem?

✓ Think logically and constructively and keep things simple. Don't be too impetuous. Avoid unnecessary pitfalls and allow time for reflection.

✓ Get accustomed to your problem-solving model, using it automatically.

✓ Don't allow your decisions to create more problems.

✓ Learn how to solve problems, just like any other skill.

2 Gathering Good Information

To understand the problem we need,
at the very least, to collect and analyse the
critical facts relevant to the situation.

5 things that really matter

1 **SEARCHING FOR INFORMATION**

2 **ASKING THE RIGHT QUESTIONS**

3 **TALKING TO PEOPLE WHO MATTER**

4 **TAPPING OTHER SOURCES**

5 **PRESENTING THE FACTS**

Before you can decide how to start solving a problem you have to go through the discipline of **gathering the facts**. It needs to be a disciplined approach because it's very tempting to skimp a bit at this stage under pressure to solve the problem. Rarely will you have time to get all the information you need. But you need at the very least to collect and analyse the **critical** facts relevant to the situation. Indeed, it's not enough just to *gather* the facts. You also have to devote sufficient time to actually understand them.

But gathering facts? That almost sounds as if we're not doing anything about the problem.

IS THIS YOU?

- *Sales of one of our products are sluggish and I need some data to tell us how badly things have fallen off and where exactly it happened.*

- *Why is the introduction of our new inventory control system two months behind schedule?* • *A major product of ours is failing in one of our customer's manufacturing facilities and we need to get it back up to speed as soon a possible.* • *That new computer system was supposed to put a stop to problems like the Leeds deliveries going to York.*

 ## SEARCHING FOR INFORMATION

It's important never to forget why you're searching for information and how that information needs to work for you.

- In the case of a **fix-it problem** the goal is to find out what is causing the problem and make it go away.

- In the case of the **do-it problem** the goal is to clarify an objective and decide how you can achieve it.

Keep the goal clearly in mind and don't stop gathering information until it has been achieved. During this part of the process, **fact-finding** has to be sharply focused. You need to know in advance what information is going to be essential and what is not. Don't move ahead on the basis of a large collection of *facts* containing little in the way of *information*.

Sniff around for information by talking informally to people in their office or over lunch, before perhaps raising the issue briefly during a team meeting. All the *details* aren't needed at this stage. What *is* required is an overview of how people and events are being affected by the problem. The details can be sorted once someone has been delegated to tackle the matter.

I sniff around for information, usually by talking informally with people – in their office, over lunch, before or after a meeting – and then perhaps raising the issue briefly during a team meeting.

It's important to figure out what the facts mean and so you must analyse their significance in relation to the problem facing you. The facts alone have little or nothing to tell you. Is it a **one-off problem**, for example, or is it a **systems problem**? A one-off problem can often be resolved by giving someone a nudge in the right direction or a nod of approval to their suggested way forward. A systems problem, on the other hand, usually involves a wider range of customer related difficulties requiring more managerial involvement, because it might have a bearing on how the whole team operates.

 ASKING THE RIGHT QUESTIONS

Fact-finding is largely a matter of asking the *right people* the *right questions*.

- **What** has happened and precisely **how** did it happen? Examine the situation from every viewpoint and arrive at an assessment with which everyone concurs.
- **Where** and **when** did the problem occur? Are the location and time factors significant?
- **Who** are the people involved in the situation and how did their involvement affect what happened? Can you expect their behaviour to change in any way?

- **why** hasn't someone sorted something out by now? Am I missing something here?

A checklist like this is useful to kick-start the problem-solving process. It should, however, become second nature once you recognise the importance of an inquiring frame of mind.

Note the magic words. **What, who, why, where** and **when** with **how** thrown in for good measure. They are the words of someone who is digging for answers, with one question leading naturally to another. More precisely, the answers you receive are **leading you somewhere**.

 TALKING TO PEOPLE WHO MATTER

Asking questions is important but it doesn't mean you have to provide all the answers yourself. The most appropriate information is usually gathered from the people involved.

- **What** happened, Jim?

- **When** did you first notice something was wrong, Alice?

- Any idea which direction, or **where**, it came from?

- **What** do you think might happen if we removed it, Sarah?

- **Who** else is involved?

- Has this had any effect on the work you do, Dave?

- **How** do things look from where you sit, Karen?

- Any idea what we should be doing about this?

- Anything I've missed?

When you systematically collect information like this you must decide in advance whom to talk to and what specific ground you want to cover with your queries.

Once people gather together around a conference table,

there are always those who become less forthcoming than they are in a one-to-one situation.

More progress is made by seeking individual opinions and observations from colleagues before going after the same information in a more formal meeting.

 TAPPING OTHER SOURCES

You should continue gathering further information until the problem is solved. What is done next depends upon the nature of the problem. If, for example, sales of one of your products are sluggish you'll need data to tell you how bad the situation is and where it's happening.

If our new inventory control system is behind schedule we can gather information by talking to people and study the project management data to see exactly what's been done so far.

Information like this should be quickly available on a computer. If you can't access it find someone who can, so you're able to stop the situation from getting any worse. You can:

- Download the appropriate data from the computer.

- Get out Bill's report and read it.

- Call a meeting of the whole team.

- Try a new model on the computer.

- Stop in at the company library to look at how others have dealt with problems like this in the past.

Talk to people. They are a resource that must never be overlooked when gathering further information. Care is needed, however, because people can sometimes distort the facts if they have their own agenda. Avoid gathering too much information and remember to be selective in what you decide to use.

 PRESENTING THE FACTS

It's impossible for most of us to be able to hold in our minds all the information required to solve a problem and think about it coherently. The key to success is to present the facts succinctly where you, and others, can understand them at a glance.

Your mind should be reserved for thinking, not used as a storage house for information.

A **force-field analysis** is a simple, but very effective, way of looking at the dynamics of a problem-solving situation and an example is illustrated below. It shows how two equal forces are acting upon the pressure to make a decision but there is uncertainty as to what should be done. Because the pressure and uncertainty are in equal, but opposite, directions – both two on a scale of one (low) to three (high) – the whole problem-solving process is brought to a halt.

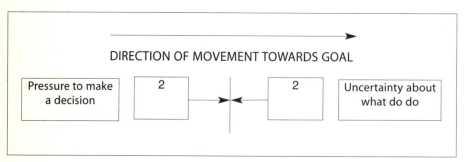

To change things, to allow the equilibrium to move to the right, you have two choices. You can up the pressure. *For God's sake, don't just stand there – make a decision!* Or you can reduce the restraining force on the right by removing the uncertainty. *That's a good idea Jim – go for it!*

The first time you do this, give **verbal instructions**. After that, **write it into the operations manual** so it will be handled routinely in future. It might be something like this:

- If re-scheduling means that shipping has to break up a full truck-load, don't do it.

- Speak to Sam, your assistant. He's been here for 17 years and he knows about these things.

- Ask the paint shop supervisor what he thinks ought to be done and, if you both agree, tell him to go ahead with it.

This analysis enables you to recognise the forces preventing you from reaching your decisions. It shows also that reducing the restraining forces is just as valid as increasing the forces that are moving you towards your goal.

There are other ways of presenting information too but how you lay them out is very important. It must keep the information you are representing in perspective with the problem you are trying to solve. It must help at a glance to guide you towards your **problem-solving goal**.

Choose a way to represent information that acts effectively to help you see things in perspective.

A **SWOT analysis** stands for **strengths, weaknesses, opportunities** and **threats**. It plays a helpful role by forcing you to put something into each of the four boxes. By doing so, it makes you aware of all the available options. When you've pinpointed the *opportunities* you want to pounce on, what threats do you have to worry about? You know your *strengths*; how about your *weaknesses*? As you can see below, the model works by simply posing questions such as these.

In many ways the best tool for laying out information is a **blank piece of paper** along with some pens and coloured markers. Lined paper is best for notes, with plain paper better for pictures and diagrams. Both are important. There's an art to note-taking. Research has shown that when done correctly it improves your recall by a factor of six because it forces you to think. It involves your intellect.

Pictures are probably the most popular means of presenting information and, when used clearly, they can capture the essence of an idea in a way that words cannot match. For example:

- A pictorial representation shows you how a number of things can be inter-connected.

- Pictures are usually better than words at presenting things *holistically.*

- Pictures allow a lot more information to be summarised on a single sheet of paper. A good 80% of text is often 'padding' that often doesn't convey any meaning.

- You don't have to flip back and forth between pages 17 and 24 as you try to relate one part of your information to another.

MAKING WHAT MATTERS WORK FOR YOU

✓ Be selective in the information you gather. Too much information often means you end up with fewer facts.

✓ You must ask the right questions of the right people to gather the relevant information. Use what, who, where, why, when **and** how **as** inquiring words.

✓ Decide in advance who you want to talk to and what specific ground you want to cover with your queries.

✓ Use the information available through colleagues, the company library, the public library, various industry associations and governmental agencies, the company computer network and, of course, the Internet.

✓ Use either a force-field analysis or a SWOT model to help with your problem-solving and fact-finding.

3 Getting to the Root of the Problem

Defining the problem is the same as understanding it – why it's there, what it's doing and what it's going to do.

5

things that
really matter

1 **IDENTIFYING THE GAP**

2 **SEPARATING SYMPTOMS AND CAUSES**

3 **IDENTIFYING THE ROOT CAUSE**

4 **USING OTHER TECHNIQUES**

5 **IDENTIFYING OUTCOMES AND CONSTRAINTS**

You now have the facts and, before you can make further progress, you have to make sure you understand the **root cause** of the problem. Defining a problem is tantamount to understanding it. Knowing why it's there and what its dynamics are and how it is likely to change between now and next week if we leave it alone. Can you draw a picture of it, with boxes and arrows that show its different components and the causal relationships between them? That's the level of understanding you should have reached by the end of this chapter. Unless you get the problem definition right, any attempt at problem-solving is futile.

So – what is the problem? What is the real problem? That is the question we have to answer.

IS THIS YOU?

● *I've got all the information needed to write my weekly column but I'm not sure exactly what to write about yet.* ● *Sales are down but we're not sure if it's a rural or an urban problem. Whether it's a decline in certain market sectors or whether our sales are down where our competitor's sales are up.* ● *Morale in our south-east shipping department is low and two people quit last week. Yet they're doing almost exactly the same work as the southern department with the same conditions and pay and there's no problem there!*

IDENTIFYING THE GAP

A **problem**, remember, is a gap between the way things are and the way they ought to be and **problem-solving** is how you close that gap. You need to understand the two sides of the gap to progress to the next step of the cycle and think how you can bridge it.

The illustration below takes a closer look at what happens in this stage, **Step Three** of the problem-solving model. You can see how the information you gathered during **Step Two** is channelled into the left hand box.

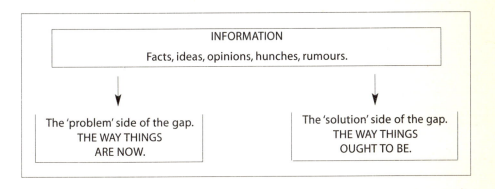

INFORMATION
Facts, ideas, opinions, hunches, rumours.

The 'problem' side of the gap.
THE WAY THINGS
ARE NOW.

The 'solution' side of the gap.
THE WAY THINGS
OUGHT TO BE.

- The box on the left represents the current state of affairs. Think of this as being the **problem** side of the gap. The *fix-it* side of the gap.
- The box on the right is for information about how things will be once you solve the problem. Think of this as being the **solution** side of the gap. The *do-it* side of the gap.

For example, a journalist is frustrated because he has so much material – all high quality stuff – that he is unable to focus on what to write in his weekly column. This is a problem for the **left-hand box**.

You then need to define the way things will be once you've solved the problem. This, of course, refers to the **right-hand box**. Using the same example again, the journalist will know the problem has been solved when the resources are filed in an orderly fashion and can be properly accessed. Information can then be processed quickly, efficiently and accurately.

Notice that, in this example, we have said the materials will be filed in an orderly manner but we haven't actually said how. That will come later. For now the priority is simply to define both sides of the gap.

To help you focus more clearly on both sides of the gap we're going to sub-divide each of the two boxes as illustrated.

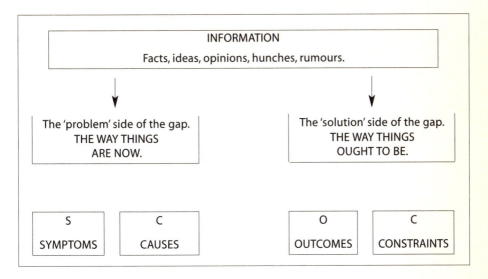

On the left you see there are now two boxes for information about the way *things are* – the **symptoms** box and the **causes** box. On the right there are two boxes for information about the way that *things will be* once the problem has been solved – the **outcomes** box and the **constraints** box.

When you think about the *problem* side of the gap, your focus will be on separating the *symptoms* from the *causes*. When you shift your attention to the *solution* side of the gap your focus will be on identifying the outcomes you want to achieve, whilst also recognising the constraints you'll have to satisfy in doing so.

 SEPARATING SYMPTOMS AND CAUSES

Here we deal mainly with the **fix-it** type of problem where its cause is normally something you have to dig for. It is often called the **root cause** because it lies beneath the surface. However, it produces the symptoms of the problem above the surface for all to see.

Let's take an example of falling sales. We shall be using some of those inquiring questions identified in Chapter 2 for our digging.

- **Where** does it occur and where does it not occur?

You need to look at sales figures right across the region and break them down into smaller chunks of information. Have sales fallen in one area, dragging the figures down for the whole region? If there's a pattern here, what is it? Maybe your sales are down in those areas where your competitor's sales are up. If so perhaps the key to your problem lies more in their sales strategies and figures rather than in your own. Again, look for a pattern.

- **When** does the problem occur and when does it not occur?

Is there a pattern here? Are sales figures up during the first half of the month but down over the last few weeks.

- **Who** is involved and who is not involved?

Is there a uniform dip in sales performance across the whole of the team? Have you always had a handful of poor performers producing poor results? Look for the pattern.

- **What** precisely is the problem and what is not the problem?

Sales are down but you must be more precise. Is it sales volume? Is it profit contribution? Is it sales within certain key product areas? If it's sales *volume* that's down then be clear about it. Has there been an absolute decline in sales or is it being measured against targets that have risen unrealistically. Maybe you're dealing with a product that is showing its age and Marketing should take responsibility for not revitalising it?

You can see that the more you dig, the trickier it might get, yet a pattern begins to emerge. If we take this example further it's possible to see how the problem might be defined. Sales are down because your customers are changing their buying habits. Their economic strategies are being driven increasingly by the parent company and the decision-making processes have become more centralised. You need to take a long, hard look at how the industry is changing and how it's going to affect your own business strategies.

So, the fact that sales are down is just a *symptom*. The real issues go a lot deeper and are to do with fundamental questions of **change**, **adaptation** and **strategy**.

 IDENTIFYING THE ROOT CAUSE

There is no single best way of getting down to the root cause of a problem but one method is to keep asking **Why?** until you run out of answers.

Bill: *I'm having problems with Jennifer.*

Liz: *A 'problem'? In what sense?*

Bill: *I just can't seem to be able to work with her.*

Liz: *Why is that?*

Bill: *She seems to have a chip on her shoulder.*

Liz: *Any idea why that is?*

Bill: *I think – I'm not sure, but I think – she wanted that job in Marketing that Joanne ended up with.*

Liz: *Why is that? Why did she want the job so badly?*

Bill: *The challenge, I suppose. It's something different. It's a good career move.*

Liz: *Why should not getting the job cause her to go around with a chip on her shoulder?*

Bill: *I think she felt she deserved it more than Joanne.*

Liz: *Why?*

Bill: *I'm not sure. I think she just felt that she was better qualified to do the job.*

Liz is pushing Bill until she gets answers. She might not be happy with the final outcome and could come back to Bill with something like this.

'For what it's worth, Bill, I think Joanne *was* the right person for that job. Marketing has changed so much in the past year and Jennifer doesn't have the skills we're looking for. More to the point, Bill, I'm not sure if Jennifer knows that. If that's the case, she needs to understand exactly what was required in the marketing job and why she didn't get it. As managers, it's our job to educate people along those lines ... Isn't it.'

This is a good example of a possible root cause turning out to be something other than you first thought, and how it was reached by asking *Why?*

When scientists want to isolate and identify the cause of a problem they compare a control group to an experimental group. You can set up the same type of comparison in the way you ask your inquiring questions.

- **Where** does the problem occur?
- **Where** does the problem not occur?
- **When** does the problem occur?
- **When** does the problem *not* occur?
- **Who** is involved in the problem situation?
- **Who** is *not* involved?
- **What** precisely is the problem?
- **What** is *not* the problem?

If the problem is, for example, that people on one team are unhappy about your overtime policy why aren't those on the other teams complaining too? Perhaps they are but aren't saying so, or maybe it's just one person who's moaning and is stirring the others to complain as well.

But perhaps the root cause of the problem is with being in that team. With the way it's being led. You don't jump to conclusions but neither do you ignore what the evidence is suggesting to you.

 USING OTHER TECHNIQUES

We've introduced the specific technique of asking the questions **why** and why **not**. Now you're going to look at a few more.

- Testing your hypotheses.
- Arguing with yourself
- Taking action – hypothetically.

Testing your hypotheses is a popular method of testing your thoughts and ideas. It suggests that *if X is the cause, then Y should hold true*. For example, if the marked decline in your export business is being caused by the sustained strength of the pound sterling, then historical data should show that your export business was strongest when sterling was at its weakest.

The idea is to play out a solution in your mind right through to the action phase and see if it solves the problem.

Arguing with yourself doesn't mean arguing between yourselves. It means you introduce a rule that every time you come up with what you consider to be the root cause of a problem, another part of you plays devil's advocate and refutes it. `Is morale low in the south-east shipping department because of low wages?' Hardly, because the team in the southern shipping department is part of the same productivity deal and there are no reported problems there.

Taking action hypothetically means you play out a solution in your mind and see whether it solves the problem. If the answer is either *no, it will not*, or *no, not necessarily*, then you should continue with your search for the real cause.

If the problem with the south-east shipping department is poor leadership, will replacing the manager produce a lift in morale? Imagine another manager in place and see if your instincts tell you there will be an improvement. Ask yourself what a new manager would do to turn things around.

Don't move ahead without treading very carefully. Unless you can make a convincing case that replacing the manager will change things for the better then you need to keep working on the definition of the problem.

We've already looked at the usefulness of **drawing a picture**. Sketching out a problem pictorially is often enough to highlight the causal relationships of a complex situation. As you develop your diagrammatic picture you will begin to get a sense of how the whole situation hangs together. You can identify causal links and where the change levers are.

 IDENTIFYING OUTCOMES AND CONSTRAINTS

In practice, this part of the process deals mainly with the *do-it* type of problem. **Outcomes** are results that your chosen solution will have to produce and **constraints** are the limits within which you will have to operate.

You identify and describe the real **outcome** in a *do-it*

situation in much the same way you would identify the root cause of a *fix-it* problem. You keep asking the **why** question until your answers have a ring of finality about them.

It's very important that you define the real objective you are trying to achieve. A good question to ask is: *What is the actual outcome we want to achieve and why is it important?*

Having been given the task of establishing a company library, one of your middle managers was surprised when the matter was raised at her annual appraisal. She thought she'd done a good job converting an empty office into a comfortably furnished and well-stocked resources area. What she hadn't realised was that no one was using it because few people knew it was there.

You must keep asking yourself exactly what outcome you want to achieve. In the library example it would have been that you want colleagues to have ready access to resources that will provide necessary market data. Your follow-up question would again be: *Why?* with the outcome being that such information would enhance individual performance and ultimately, increase output.

Identifying the desired outcome in this way is important. The appropriate mindset will have a real bearing on the way the person approaches the project and, therefore, affect the outcome of your *do-it* problem.

Using the library example again, your **constraints** might have been to develop the library but:

- to have it done by the end of the month

- not to spend more than £1,000

- not to knock any walls down.

Constraints are usually limits of:

- time

- space

- money

- materials

- people.

   Constraints may also involve limits on the range of acceptable solutions.

- The solution has to be acceptable to the directors because it needs their approval.

- The projected increase in profit contribution should be at least 15%.

- The design of the product has to be consistent with standards being introduced by our US parent.

MAKING WHAT MATTERS WORK FOR YOU

✓ You must know why a problem is there and make sure you define it precisely. Your task at this stage is to identify and describe the two sides of the gap – the way things are now (symptoms **and** causes) and the way you want them to be (outcomes **and** constraints).

✓ Use the inquiring questions: What, who, why, where, when **and** how, to gather precise information on the symptoms and causes of the problem.

✓ When seeking to identify the root cause of a problem you must keep asking the question *Why?* and don't give up until you run out of answers. You can also compare why a problem occurred in one place and why it didn't occur in another. Be ready if the root cause turns out to be something other than you first thought.

✓ Think of your ideas as being hypotheses that can be tested. If X is the cause then Y should hold true. You can also argue propositions with yourself by playing out a solution in your mind to identify causal links and possible change levers.

✓ Define the outcome you want to achieve. Identify the constraints – usually of time, space, money, materials and people, but can also include changes in company policy.

4 Raising the Options

You've gathered the facts and understand the problem.
The quality of your ultimate solution, however, will
only be as high as the quality of solution options you raise.

5

things that
really matter

1 **EXAMINING ALL AVAILABLE SOLUTIONS**

2 **ASKING QUESTIONS**

3 **EXPLORING COMMON PITFALLS**

4 **THINKING STRATEGICALLY**

5 **DEVELOPING A SINGLE OPTION**

The problem has been defined to your satisfaction and you are now ready to seek some options that you hope will provide a solution. This will not be easy. If the solution was obvious someone would have implemented it by now and solved the problem. Make sure that the options you generate cover all the angles and that you examine each one thoroughly before making a decision.

So now we're ready to move on to that portion of the problem-solving cycle where the **solution**, not the problem, takes the spotlight. And the quality of the solution we ultimately select will only be as high as the quality of the **solution options** we generate and examine.

IS THIS YOU?

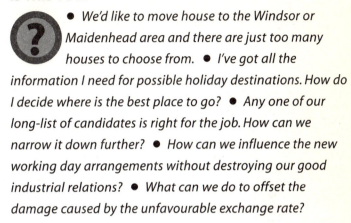

● We'd like to move house to the Windsor or Maidenhead area and there are just too many houses to choose from. ● I've got all the information I need for possible holiday destinations. How do I decide where is the best place to go? ● Any one of our long-list of candidates is right for the job. How can we narrow it down further? ● How can we influence the new working day arrangements without destroying our good industrial relations? ● What can we do to offset the damage caused by the unfavourable exchange rate?

Ⓘ EXAMINING ALL AVAILABLE SOLUTIONS

Make sure, before you go on, that every solution worthy of consideration is available to you. Here are some guidelines that will help you in your quest.

Make sure you **focus on feasibility**. There is no point in considering options that are beyond the resources at your disposal. Only consider options that can be implemented within the constraints of your situation and promise to deliver the outcomes you've targeted. For example, when dealing with what you might think is a trivial problem, telling the customer to push off is not a workable option.

Reduce it to **two alternatives** if you can. By moving from the many options *available* to those that are *feasible* means you'll have eliminated many from your list. But there's still a lot to do. Ideally you should reduce it to a choice between *two* feasible options. Three is acceptable if this is too difficult, but don't go beyond that number.

Narrowing it down to two options that are attractive and will get the job done is most desirable. Two candidates for the job. Two possible sites for a distribution centre or two formats for the proposal.

There are occasions when you shouldn't neglect the **do-nothing** option. Deciding not to decide is a valid option. You might consider the problem is not worth solving, or that it will solve itself, or now is not the best time to do something about it. More importantly, you might consider that meddling will make matters worse. This option doesn't literally mean doing nothing or avoiding the problem. You could:

- **Monitor the situation** if the problem is not urgent.
- **Treat the symptoms** if they demand an urgent response even if now isn't the time to tackle the root cause.
- Make a **temporary decision** if you have to, in order to buy time.
- Make a **conditional decision**. Decide what to do but don't implement it until you're sure a decision is needed.

Don't be afraid to **think creatively** when the need arises. This means you consider a feasible solution from a range of options that fall outside the boundary lines you unconsciously drew around the problem. You're challenging your own presumptions and considering options, for a number of reasons, that you might not normally contemplate.

Creative thinking isn't just a matter of brainstorming. It means releasing your mind from the shackles and boundaries which prevent if from wandering too far afield.

Be confident enough to ask questions that might seem too obvious to be worth asking. For example:

- Is this problem worth solving?
- Is it really a problem?
- What if we forget the whole thing and go back to work?

- What if we launched the product anyway?

Having said that, looking for **logic** in the situation is probably more important than being creative. Allow the logic inherent in the problem itself to suggest the appropriate solution. If, for example, the main issue is poor communications between Engineering and Logistics then you need to break down the barriers between the two before you do anything else.

 ASKING QUESTIONS

There are some questions that will help you ensure that all options worth looking at have been considered.

Always ask what did we do the last time?. If you've solved this problem before don't presume that you should do the same thing again, but *do* consider it as an option.

Keep these points in mind:

- The two situations may look the same but they can contain some very subtle differences.
- What worked last time may not work as well this time.
- There's always a chance that you chose the wrong solution last time but it just happened to work.
- There's a good chance that what you did last time was an adequate solution but not an optimal one.

If our major competitors have faced the same problem then it makes sense to find out as much as we can about what they did to solve it and why.

Find out **how your competitors dealt with this problem**. You'll need to be geared up for this type of information gathering. If you don't have a contact in the competitor's camp then figure out how to cultivate one. Organise someone to clip newspaper articles and reports on comparable companies. Get someone to read their chairman's book and report back to you.

Ask yourself whether the options you're examining **will actually solve the problem**. Options have to be *explored*, not just identified. It's worth taking a few minutes to think each one through carefully. This makes it clearer in your mind and you can visualise what each option might actually do for you in practice.

 EXPLORING COMMON PITFALLS

Three common pitfalls often emerge when your attention turns to the development of solution options. Be aware of each one.

The most common pitfall is **not considering all the options**. Make sure you take the time to explore and develop all possibilities. Don't allow an emphasis on decision-making, or pressure to get the problem solved immediately, deter you from properly examining the options. Don't make the mistake of thinking that information gathering is not as important as decision-making.

Don't worry too much at this stage about searching for the right **solution,** as this will often blind you to other possibilities. What you need are solutions that will *really work*. They don't have to be perfect. They just need to be realistic, workable and manageable.

Another common pitfall is **sticking with the tried and true** when something more exciting and effective may be available. When you're under pressure for immediate results this may often seem a simple remedy. It is fine for the short term but is no answer to recurring problems.

 THINKING STRATEGICALLY

Be careful of moving from goal-setting to action-taking without developing a general **strategy**. A good way of doing this is to think backwards. **Visualise** the end result you desire and work backwards to see how you got there. By adopting this strategy you're *defining* the space in which your solution can be searched for and developed. Most of us do this anyway but fail to recognise it as a valid aspect of the problem-solving process.

A good example is planning a holiday. You know when you're going but haven't decided where to go. You don't gather information from scores of travel brochures because you've already considered what type of vacation you want. You work backwards from that point because it saves so much time.

Thinking strategically means that there's less likelihood of sweating your way up a ladder only to find that you've positioned it against the wrong wall.

Thinking strategically also helps get things right because you ask yourself whether you need a *quick* or an *optimal* solution. Is it something you can deal with instantly or should you call a meeting of the whole team to tackle it in a more planned fashion? By adopting this approach you not only save valuable time but you're more likely to find workable solutions.

DEVELOPING A SINGLE OPTION

At first glance this might seem to be a contradiction of what we've already covered. But the fact is that you shouldn't ignore the possibility of **developing a single option**, because it can be the best way forward. Sometimes you have to struggle with a single solution option until, after a lot of re-working, testing and refining, it brings you to a satisfactory conclusion.

Never be afraid to do what's best for you. If that means pursuing a single option instead of looking at a range of them, then go for it.

MAKING WHAT MATTERS WORK FOR YOU

✓ Examine the full range of solutions available. Make sure that they are feasible and that they can be reduced to a manageable number. If necessary, don't be afraid of the 'do nothing' option. Think creatively but also seek the logic in the situation before committing yourself.

✓ Ask yourself whether what you did last time will work again or is this situation different? Don't waste time solving it yourself if someone else has already done it. Get some of your people to check up on your competitors if you think they've cracked it.

✓ Take the time to consider all the options but don't spend too long searching for the 'right' solution. A common pitfall is sticking with the tried and true. Be more inspirational in your approach but remember that solutions must be workable.

✓ Think backwards from your visualised end result to give you an instant focus of what to do next. Ask questions that address each step of your strategy until they lead to a satisfactory solution.

✓ Examining a range of options isn't always necessary. If appropriate, develop a single option by re-working, testing and refining it until it evolves into a satisfactory solution.

5 Choosing the Best Solution

You've laid out a series of options,
all designed to solve the problem,
and the task now is to choose the best one.

5
things that really matter

1 **REACHING AN EFFECTIVE DECISION**

2 **DECIDING HOW TO DECIDE**

3 **TAKING THE LOGICAL ROUTE**

4 **RELYING ON YOUR INSTINCTS**

5 **AVOIDING PITFALLS WHEN SELECTING YOUR SOLUTION**

You're at the stage where a decision has to be made and it is here that your judgement, business sense and intuition come into play. You have to choose an option that might not be scientifically, logically or theoretically best, but is the most practical and realistic available.

The test of a decision is whether or not it delivers the goods. Whether it **solves the problem**.

Get the process right. That is a mantra that you should repeat to yourself over and over again until you get sick of hearing it.

IS THIS YOU?

● *My boss has told me to organise a video-conference between the parent US company, our European partners and us. Where do I start?*

● *I've been asked to make some important stock market investments. How should I go about it?* ● *Harry says there is no way he can initiate the new IT network by the end of the year yet we can't develop our new customer database without it.* ● *Helen has just been head hunted by a major competitor and she's been responsible for developing our new Middle-East products. What can we do?*

 REACHING AN EFFECTIVE DECISION

An **effective decision**, or an effective solution, is one that accomplishes the intended result. There are several strategies for achieving this and all should be used concurrently.

You must **get the process right**. Bad decisions occur because of a weakness in the problem-solving cycle. A slight miscalculation can easily result in you choosing a solution that turns out to be sub-optimal.

Testing out your decision, mentally, will focus your mind on the practical details and it's also a good way to look at the risks that might be involved. Sketching out an action plan in this way enables you to test your solution before committing yourself to it.

Sometimes you can actually **test your decision in practice**, for example, by putting a new IT system in one part of the factory to see how well it works. If a decision has to be approved by other people, try testing it on one or two key people before submitting it. That way you go into a meeting much better equipped to argue your case and come away with a positive result.

Never make a decision in isolation. **Talk it through** with at least one person or write it down for someone to read and give you valuable feedback.

Get the right people involved because they can provide sound, authoritative advice. By doing this you also give them a sense of ownership which, in turn, will encourage greater commitment to your project. Think this one through carefully. Whose commitment will be essential and when, exactly, should they be involved?

There are always pitfalls in most decision-making situations and you need to **assess and cover the risks** very carefully by asking:

- What can go wrong?

- What are the chances of *that* happening?

- How serious would the consequences be?

- What steps would we take to deal with them?

- Can we reduce the likelihood of it happening?

- What is the worst possible thing that could happen?

- Are we prepared to live with that?

Answer the question *'What's the worst possible thing that can happen?'* in some detail and then the issue becomes *'Are we prepared to live with that?'* The real question might be whether you and your client can actually absorb the worst case scenario.

You need to get the **timing right**. The world moves faster every day and, although decisions don't necessarily have to be made on a quicker basis than before, the whole problem-solving process needs to be attuned to the speed of change.

- Don't get bogged down in data analysis. Let the IT section do it.

- Make sure your intelligence network is working for you. You must know what's happening in the industry at large.

- You can't afford the cost of delay so eliminate all forms of procrastination.

To cope with this increasing pressure your sensitivity and awareness of potential problems has to be sharper and more effective than ever before.

Don't let decisions become rules. In other words, don't allow a solution to a problem to become routine practice without testing its effectiveness. If you've got a parcel that has to be with a client tomorrow but you've missed the post then you call a courier. This might well become a routine as there are few alternatives. But ask why the parcel missed the post in the first place and you begin to question other decisions that led to this solution.

The trouble begins when we make routine the things that shouldn't be routinised – when we allow routines to become a substitute for thinking.

 DECIDING HOW TO DECIDE

It is often useful to talk through the general strategy you will use in making a decision. If you're hiring someone, for example, do you:

- State you're going to hire the first candidate who can do the job.

- Want the best possible person for the job even if you have to interview fifty people.

- Seek the attitudes of enthusiasm, desire and commitment in the knowledge that you can teach the technical skills of the job.

- Refuse to hire anyone who doesn't have the potential for growth into other types of work within the company.

It's difficult to argue that one strategy is better than the others but by talking about it you are making it a conscious part of the decision-making process.

 TAKING THE LOGICAL ROUTE

You can take a **logical route** to help you in this part of the cycle by listing those criteria you think are important for the job and giving them measurable values. The example below can be used for hiring someone. You can adapt it to any situation you wish.

		Larkin		Jones		Stevens	
	V	**R**	**VR**	**R**	**VR**	**R**	**VR**
Education	1	3	3	3	3	2	2
Learning	2	2	4	1	2	1	2
People skills	2	1	2	2	4	1	2
Brightness	2	3	6	2	4	2	4
Knowledge	1	2	2	3	3	2	2
Attitude	**3**	**2**	**6**	**3**	**9**	**2**	**6**
TOTAL			**23**		**25**		**18**

On the left you'll see a list of criteria starting with education and finishing with attitude. Next to it is the **V** column that represents a **value** for each criterion, on a scale of one to three, according to the importance you place upon it for the job. Here we think **attitude** is important so we give it a value of **three**. Knowledge is not so important so it gets a value of one.

Next you **rate** the candidates in column **R**, again on a scale of one to three. For example, Larkin's **attitude** could have been better so we give him a value of **two**. By multiplying the figure in each candidate's **R** column by the figure in the corresponding **V** column we get their score against each criterion and put it in their **VR** column. Here we see Larkin's attitude score is six (3 × 2) whereas Jones' attitude score is better at nine (3 × 3).

Add all the scores in the **VR** column for each candidate and you see how well they meet the criteria you consider are important for the job. In the example above Jones achieves the best overall score.

 ### RELYING ON YOUR INSTINCTS

Another way that you can make a decision in the hiring example above is to reflect quietly on the requirements of the job and visualise each candidate, in turn, actually doing the work. You can combine this, if you wish, with the grid illustrated above but the the key here is that you use your instincts about the candidate to make the final decision.

It's important to remember that with the instinctive approach you are relying upon your judgement and judgement is nearly always acquired through experience.

Relying on instincts can be a more uncertain method of making a decision. However, if you're sufficiently experienced, it can often produce dividends through identifying *hidden talent* that cannot be identified or measured by the use of grids or questionnaires.

AVOIDING PITFALLS WHEN SELECTING YOUR SOLUTION

Don't make the mistake at this stage of thinking that you've done the toughest bit and selecting the solution will be easy. There are **pitfalls** that might well undermine the good work you've already put in place.

Quite often you think you can **decide without deciding**. You might decide, for example, not to do anything for the moment. However, by choosing this as a solution you are still giving the situation the full force of a decision, which carries with it certain consequences. Because you think you've made a decision you might relax, or even forget about it for a while. Your competitors, however, will still be active and could well take advantage of opportunities you, perhaps unwittingly, choose to ignore by making a non-decision. You will have lost the chance to make a proactive decision and influence matters as a result.

Never **regard a decision as *final*** by closing down the problem-solving cycle, under the assumption that a decision has been made. You might have made a decision last week but the world has changed and could end up with a worse problem than you started with. Don't think that changing your mind is a sign of weakness. To be a good manager you should monitor things and not be afraid to re-activate the whole problem-solving cycle if you think it's necessary.

In this world of continuous and rapid change we need to treat decisions as open-ended and subject them to constant review.

Although it is important to use your instincts when making decisions **don't rely too heavily on your *gut feelings*** as they can be misleading. You might have a *hunch* about something, but don't let it override common sense or the advice of colleagues or specialists who might not share your opinion. There is a time and a place for instincts but don't be ruled by them.

Tunnel vision is often a pitfall, so make sure you look at the big picture. Don't choose an option that satisfies the immediate criteria but falls short of meeting the demands or constraints of the longer-term problem. For example, it's easy to rush into a job with a growing company that offers a great salary along with a BMW but think about what you'll be doing in 12 months time. Will you have the same chances of career development in the big league, or will you be a glorified sales rep working all hours scratching around in the second division? If you're good at what you do then you'll want to compete at the highest level.

MAKING WHAT MATTERS WORK FOR YOU

✓ To make an effective decision you must get the timing and the process right and get the appropriate people involved from the outset. Test out your decision mentally and then practise it in a small, controlled situation so you can assess and cover the risks involved. Avoid letting past decisions become rules without testing their effectiveness in new situations.

✓ Talk through the general strategy you plan to adopt in making the decision. Make it a *conscious* part of the process.

✓ Use a grid that attaches criteria and measurable values to the decisions you have to make.

✓ Don't be afraid to use your instincts as part of the decision-making process but remember the importance of combining them with experience.

✓ Avoid the pitfalls that are always present when choosing a solution. Be wary of the consequences of making a non-decision and always be prepared to change your decision. Don't rely totally on your gut feelings and make sure you look at the big picture.

6 Getting It Solved

*Your problem is solved when your
decision is translated into effective action,
the results monitored and the
problem situation re-assessed.*

Your decision, by itself, will not solve the problem. You need
to translate it into an effective plan of action and execute it.

- What, specifically, is the goal of the proposed action?

- What action steps are involved?

- What's the schedule?

- Who is responsible for monitoring and expediting those
  steps?

- Who has to be involved at each step along the way?

- What resources will be needed?

- What intelligence will be needed?

- What costs will be involved?

- Who is responsible for managing the total
  implementation cycle?

- Who is accountable for the project?

- Is everyone on board?

IS THIS YOU?

- *Your boss has asked you to implement your agreed changes to resolve the problems in the Packaging Department but where do you start?*
- *You've decided what to do about the mail order department restructuring but you're uncertain about the costings on one part of the project.* • *You need someone from the factory floor to put an action plan into operation and then monitor results for the next three months.* • *Rumour has it that Harry, your finance manager, is opposed to your action plan. Should you try to turn him around?*

 BUILDING A VISUAL PLAN

To help you work through the sequence of events and spot potential conflicts you should devise a **visual action plan**. It might include breaking your total solution down into major *action* chunks and plotting them on a planning calendar as illustrated below.

You might prefer a flow chart that shows how the various steps of your solution will link up and overlap, or

T	W	Th	F	M	T	W	Th	F	M	T	W	Th	F	M	T	W
29	30	1	2	5	6	7	8	9	12	13	14	15	16	19	20	21
Report of Surveys																
				Data analysis												
						Report Draft										
									Report							
											Review Sessions					

you might consider that a simple schedule of events will do.
Like the whole problem-solving model, you must decide
what's best for you and try it in practice.

*You need to keep the action plan as simple as possible but complex
and flexible enough to do the job.*

To compose a visual plan you should:

- Identify your objective.
- Structure the major chunks of your activity into an
  activity that has an identifiable beginning and end.
- Define a goal for each chunk.
- Attach a target date for each activity.
- Develop an action plan for each goal.

First you must **define your objective**. That means you
must identify what end result your solution has to
accomplish and by what date.

Then **identify the major chunks** of your solution into an
activity that has a clear beginning and end. Your data
analysis, for example, starts on the 5th and finishes on the
8th. All the action parts, when strung together, should
reflect the successful completion of the whole project.

It is useful too, to **define a goal for each chunk** of your
activities. Each goal should be a significant milestone, which
means that something tangible is produced from that
chunk and passed along the process. The survey reports, for
example, will initiate the data analysis, and so on.

Once your goals have been defined it is important that
you **attach a target date to each one** to ensure the project
is completed on time. This might require some juggling with
priorities and a few deals with other departments, but get it
done as it's important.

Label		
Goal		
	Action	Deadline
1		
2		
3		
4		
5		
6		

To ensure smooth progress you should **develop an action plan for each goal** on a separate form like the one illustrated below. This will help you break down each goal into its component action steps with each step being assigned its own specific target date. By writing it down in this way it will guide your day-to-day, hour-by-hour activities. Six action steps are listed here, but, again, you can adapt them to your own circumstances.

 LEARNING THE ART OF DELEGATION

The art of successful **delegation** relies heavily on the principle of **leverage** which literally means multiplying your impact. You can best maximise your value by identifying and developing solutions rather than implementing them. Making a decision that affects how ten people will go about their job, for example, is a high leverage activity.

There are two classes of activity in which you should be engaged:

- Activities that have a widespread impact extending beyond your own personal work.

- Activities that require your unique managerial perspective and status.

You should also remember that decisions about problem-solving are best delegated to those closest to the action, not only because their knowledge will be useful, but because the all important team effort will be enhanced by their involvement.

Your delegation should follow three simple rules, **the first being delegating by results.** This means you don't give people **tasks** to do – you give them a **result to achieve**.

- Make sure you clarify the objective and the date by which it must be achieved.

- Spell out when you should be consulted or when their initiative should be exercised.

- Give the people your *feel* for the problem in hand.

- Tell them you want a plan of action showing how expected results will be accomplished.

- Make sure they have the necessary authority to be able to carry out the delegated assignment.

Once you have delegated by these rules don't meddle. Nothing communicates more clearly that you don't have confidence in your colleagues than interfering with what they're doing.

Do spot checks by asking very explicit questions which require fairly detailed responses. That way you get a picture of whether the person is on top of things.

The second rule is building in controls. You want people to work independently, but you must also exercise your ultimate responsibility for the work by using a system of checks and controls.

- Build in action plans, deadlines, periodic progress reports, and so on.
- Arrange periodic meetings to discuss and evaluate progress.
- Follow up on a few tasks to see they've been done properly.
- Keep yourself available for help if it's needed. Be prepared to step in if necessary.
- *But* – always judge by results and not by the way they were achieved.

The third rule is that you must monitor and follow up. You might want to use the Quality Assurance method of *spot checking* to monitor how a delegated project is being carried out. Or you might prefer to review the rough draft of an early report before someone has polished off the rough edges. If you do, remember the importance of approving what the person plans to do and their thinking behind the decisions rather than the way it is executed.

Monitoring and following up isn't meddling. It's part of you displaying your perfectly legitimate managerial role as a **delegator.**

 MAXIMISING YOUR CHANCES

When you propose a solution you're competing for scarce resources. Others will make decisions in terms of giving you time, money, equipment and people to get the job done. Here are a few guidelines to help you get those decisions made in your favour.

You must **focus on today's priorities, not yesterday's**. If you were given a task two months ago make sure it's still a priority today. Check, almost daily, to make sure the issue hasn't shifted in some subtle way and that the priority hasn't changed.

Make sure you **get the key people involved**. Anyone whose enthusiasm and diligent execution is crucial to success should be involved from the earliest opportunity, and as extensively as possible.

Preparation is the single, most important step you can take in working towards a successful presentation.

It is very important that you **polish your presentation skills**. Your successful presentation relies on your disciplined attention to some practical tasks beforehand, as well as requiring you to be confident and polished in all you say and do.

- Decide upon your goal for the presentation and what you think each member of the audience will want to take away with them.

- Find out what role those present at the presentation play in the decision-making process and think through exactly what key concepts you want to implant in their minds.

- Think through people's current perceptions with regard to the action you want them to take as a result of your presentation.

- Identify what the audience will need to learn during, or after, the presentation if they are to accept your recommendations.

- Think through, and prepare for, the queries, concerns or challenges you might need to deal with.

- Identify the style of presentation and communication that will best allow your goal to be achieved.

 MAKING THINGS HAPPEN

The rule here is that **things won't happen unless you make them happen**. If it's your problem, and therefore your solution, then you're the one who has to champion the idea and spearhead the change. Ignore this rule and even the soundest and most exciting of ideas is likely to fall by the wayside after the initial flurry of interest and activity.

If you've been asked to produce an employee newsletter, for example, you've got to make sure there's something in it that people want to read. It's one thing researching how to produce one, getting to the mock-up stage successfully and using it to get people's input, but it's another matter to then drive the project on to attracting a broad readership.

 LEARNING FROM YOUR RESULTS

The question you must ask yourself now is **whether your solution has worked to resolve your problem**. You ask this whether your efforts to solve the problem have been successful, partially successful, or a dismal failure. By doing so you are returning to Step One, the problem awareness stage of the model, to see if you still have a problem to solve. If one still exists you must gather facts and information about the new situation and progress from there again. It might well be that, with hindsight, you'll see that you didn't solve the problem in the most efficient and effective way possible.

Did you use your time and the resources available to their best advantage? Did you consider the full range of possible solutions before deciding which one to move ahead with?

If you want to be a top performer you must always question your decisions and scrutinise your actions. This will set you apart from the average person because you'll be hungry for feedback on how you can constantly improve *your* performance.

Problem-solving, like any other skill, is something you will advance with the more you do it. Learn to tackle it with confidence but with sufficient humility to understand you might be able to do it better next time.

MAKING WHAT MATTERS WORK FOR YOU

✓ Build a simple visual action plan that defines your objective and gives clear goals for each part of the plan.

✓ To delegate successfully you should employ the principle of leverage to maximise your value and exercise it on those closest to the action. You should observe the three rules of delegating by results, building in controls and following up what's happening.

✓ You should maximise your chances of success by focusing on today's priorities, getting the key people involved and polishing your presentation skills.

✓ It's your problem and your solution so champion it and spearhead the challenge.

✓ Check whether your solution has actually solved the problem by going back to Step One of the problem-solving model. To be a top performer you must question your decisions, scrutinise your actions and always invite feedback.